California Mission Guide

Bob Nicholson

CaliforniaMissionGuide.com

Table of Contents

The California Mission Story

The California missions represented the final expansion of the Spanish Empire. From 1769 to 1823, Spanish soldiers and monks built a total of 21 Missions and 5 Presidios (or military forts), stretching North from Mexico, along the Pacific coast, through the territory that was then known as Alta California.

With the Mexican revolt, which culminated in Mexico's independence in 1821, the Spanish presence in North America came to an end. In 1824, the expansion of the Mission system was halted. The missions were secularized in 1833, bringing an end to a critical chapter in California's history (most of the missions were later returned to the Catholic Church).

Over a short period – little more than 50 years – the Spanish brought a new culture to California, spreading European religion, agricultural practices, and eventually forms of government. Together, the missions performed over 87,000 baptisms, and 24,000 marriages. The mission communities kept over 150,000 cattle, and grew 150,000,000 pounds of wheat.

Sadly, European diseases, carried by the settlers, killed thousands of California Indians. This, along with military victories of the Spanish over natives, established permanent dominance of European civilization.

The settlements around the missions became the seeds of modern California's major cities. The trail connecting the missions, El Camino Real, became California's first "highway," and its route is closely followed by modern Highway 101.

The designs of the missions still influence California architecture.

In a very real sense, California as we know it today would not exist without the foundation of the missions.

Secularization

In 1834, the government of Mexico ordered the secularization of the missions. The mission buildings and the surrounding lands were removed from control of the church and turned over to the Indians who had served the missions. Sadly, the Indians were ill prepared to deal with the complexity of modern society, and for the most part they quickly lost control of the lands to speculators and thieves.

Although many of the missions were later returned to the Catholic Church, secularization brought an effective end to the age of the California missions.

The Missions Today

Today, all 21 of the mission sites can be visited, and most are still in use as churches.

Unfortunately, almost all the missions are in serious need of repair. Some are in ruins, and several are close to collapse. A few have been restored or entirely rebuilt, and one is a California State historical park.

Regardless of their state of repair, a visit to a California mission provides a fascinating look into California's early history.

The Presidios

The 21 California missions were established by the *Franciscan Order of the Catholic Church* in order to spread their faith throughout California. However, the building of the missions was strongly supported by the Spanish government, which saw in the missions a way to expand the Spanish sphere of influence.

Each mission formed the core of a settlement, many of which eventually grew into California's major cities. The missions were protected by small contingents of soldiers.

These small detachments were not sufficient to secure Spain's interests in Alta California. The Spanish feared that other countries – especially Russia – had designs on its North American territories. In addition, there was a constant fear of pirates raiding the coastal missions and settlements. The Spanish government therefore divided Alta California into four military districts, each controlled and protected by a military fort, or presidio.

Later, after Mexico declared its independence from Spain, a fifth presidio was built at Sonoma. This presidio became the headquarters for the Mexican army in California, and the other presidios were reduced to small garrisons.

The five presidios, in order of their construction, were:

El Presidio Real de San Diego

San Diego - July 16, 1769

The first of the presidios, it formed the base for Spain's expansion into California. It was ultimately responsible for the defense of the missions at San Diego, San Luis Rey, San Juan Capistrano, and San Gabriel.

El Presidio Real de San Carlos de Monterey

Monterey - June 3, 1770

Responsible for the defense of the missions at San Luis Obispo, San Miguel, San Antonio, Soledad, San Carlos, and San Juan Bautista.

El Presidio Real de San Francisco

San Francisco - December 17, 1776

Responsible for the defense of the missions at Santa Cruz, San José, Santa Clara, San Francisco, San Rafael, and Solano.

El Presidio Real de Santa Bárbara

Santa Barbara - April 12, 1782

Responsible for the defense of the missions at San Fernando, San Buenaventura, Santa Barbara, Santa Inés, and La Purísima.

El Presidio de Sonoma

Sonoma - 1810

The final presidio, at Sonoma, was built after Mexican independence from Spain. It was intended to act as a military buffer against Russian settlements, which had reached as far south as Fort Ross. The Sonoma presidio became the headquarters of the Mexican Army in California, while the remaining presidios were abandoned and, in time, fell into ruins.

Asistencias and Estancias

Many of the California Missions had extensions, or sub-missions (*asistencias*), or ranchos (*estancias*), created to extend the reach of the missions and serve a larger community.

At one time, there were plans to form an inland chain of missions, possibly starting with the asistencias, to parallel the 21 coastal missions. The plans never materialized, and little remains of the asistencias. In fact, very few records of the asistencias survive.

Known asistencias, in order of their construction, include:

Santa Margarita de Cortona

Location: Rancho Santa Margarita, CA (not open to the public)

Founded: 1787

Santa Margarita de Cortona, was a sub-mission of Mission San Luis Obispo de Tolosa.

Some of the foundations and walls of the original structures have been incorporated into a barn and ranch house that are still in use today.

San Antonio de Pala Asistencia

Location: 3015 Pala Mission Road, Pala, CA

Founded: June 13, 1816

San Antonio de Pala was a sub-mission of Mission San Luis Rey de Francia.

The Pala Asistencia is still in use as an active Catholic church, serving the nearby Pala Indian Reservation.

Santa Ysabel Asistencia

Location: 23013 California 79, Santa Isabel, CA

Founded: September 20, 1818

Santa Ysabel was a sub-mission of Mission San Diego de Alcalá.

There is nothing left of the original asistencia. The current chapel, shown above, was constructed in 1924. There is also a small historical museum on the site.

Las Flores (San Pedro) Asistencia

Location: Camp Pendleton Marine Base, CA (not open to the public)

Founded: 1823

San Antonio de Pala, along with San Antonio de Pala (above), was a sub-mission of Mission San Luis Rey de Francia.

Las Flores consisted of a tile roofed adobe, a chapel, a hostel, and ranch buildings. All that remains are crumbling adobe bricks.

California Registered Historical Landmark No. 616

From 1823 to the 1840's the tile-roofed adobe chapel and hostel at Las Flores, built by Father Antonio Peyri, served as the asistencia to Mission San Luis Rey and provided comfort to travelers on El Camino Real. The adobe structure and adjacent corral were the site of the April 1838 battle between Juan Bautista Alvarado and Carlos Antonio Carrillo contesting the provincial governorship of Alta California.

San Bernardino Asistencia

Location: 26930 Barton Road, Redlands, CA

Founded: 1830

There is some debate about the status of this complex. It may have been a sub-mission of Mission San Gabriel, although it may have been a simple estancia, or ranch.

The current structure on the site is a reconstruction, based on San Antonio de Pala Asistencia. There is also a small museum.

California Registered Historical Landmark No. 42

This branch of San Gabriel Mission was constructed about 1830 on the San Bernardino Rancho. During the 1840s, its buildings were used by José del Carmen Lugo as part of his rancho grant. Later, after its sale to the Mormons, it was occupied by Bishop Tenney in the 1850s, and by Dr. Benjamin Barton in the 1860s. Its restoration was completed in 1937 by the Works Progress Administration, assisted by the San Bernardino County Historical Society.

Adobe: Building Bricks of the Missions

In a very real sense, the humble *adobe brick* made the California missions possible.

Although other building materials were used when available - wood for doors, roof frames, and outbuildings, or stone for chapels – adobe was available almost everywhere. Adobe had the additional advantage of being cheap, although making and building with adobe bricks required a great deal of labor.

Adobe bricks were made by combining naturally occurring clay with sand and organic material like straw or dung to bind the bricks while drying. The adobe mixture was pressed into simple wooden forms to form bricks, which were then dried in the sun.

The bricks could be used to build thick, strong walls that helped to keep the mission buildings cool in summer and warm in winter. The bricks were joined together with adobe mud, or with *lime mortar* made from limestone and seashells.

Because the bricks could be dissolved by water, the walls were protected from rain by coating them with plaster (made from sand and lime), or more adobe (which needed to be refreshed regularly). Mission architecture also featured roofs that extended well beyond the walls of the buildings, providing shaded walkways, and also providing additional protection for the walls.

The adobe clay could also be forms into roof tiles and baked in a *kiln* (a specially built oven that could reach high temperatures). When baked in the kiln, the adobe tiles *vitrified* into true ceramics, and became strong, durable, and water proof.

Not all of the missions had the skills or materials necessary to produce baked adobe ceramics. Those that did often produced roof tiles, floor tiles, bowls, jars, and cups, which they sold or traded.

Some of the missions even used adobe pipes to carry water for irrigation.

According to records at the time, the first roofing tiles were made at Mission San Antonio de Padua.

Mission San Luis Obispo further refined the process. At San Luis Obispo, horses were kept walking in circles to mix the adobe clay with their hooves.

Although adobe construction was essential to the growth of the mission system, it also a serious drawback. Adobe does not hold up well in earthquakes, and many mission structures were destroyed by earthquake damage over the years.

El Camino Real, The Royal Road

El Camino Real – "the Royal Road" – is inextricably linked to the history of California's missions. The 600-mile trail, stretching from *Mission San Diego de Alcalá* in San Diego to *Mission San Francisco Solano* in Sonoma, was created by the Spanish to link the 21 California missions and the associated settlements and presidios. Missions were located approximately 30 miles apart – a long day's ride on horseback.

The route was a continuation of the *Baja California* mission trail, and expanded Northward as the Spanish colonized California (or as it was then known, *Alta California*).

The "royal road" was in fact a modest dirt footpath. As the mission system grew and traffic increased, the simple trail became a dirt road wide enough to accommodate carts and wagons.

The first portion was not paved until 1912, when a small section in the San Francisco Bay Area became the first paved highway in California.

Technically, any road that came under the jurisdiction of the Spanish viceroys was designated a "Royal Road," and so today there are roads throughout Mexico and the southwestern United States, including California, Arizona, New Mexico, and Texas, known as *El Camino Real*.

However, in 1959 the California State Assembly recognized the historic importance of the mission trail, and designated several sections of state highway and connecting roads as the official route of El Camino Real.

In 2001, the State Assembly modified the officially recognized route (Assembly Bill 1707, Chapter 739). The official definition, from the California Streets and Highways Code, Chapter 2, Article 3, Section 635, states:

State highway routes embracing portions of Routes 280, 82, 238, 101, 5, 72, 12, 37, 121, 87, 162, 185, 92, and 123 and connecting city streets and county roads thereto, and extending in a continuous route from Sonoma southerly to the international border and near the route historically known as El Camino Real shall be known and designated as "El Camino Real."

Long before its official recognition, the road was unofficially commemorated by a private group, El Camino Real Association, with a series of bronze bells placed along the route. The cast bells we suspended from 11-foot high posts designed to resemble a shepherd's crook. The first of the bells was unveiled August 15, 1906 at the Plaza Church in the Pueblo near Olvera Street in Los Angeles.

Without official support, and only sporadic maintenance, the bells fell in disrepair; many were vandalized or stolen.

In 2000, a federal grant was obtained for the restoration of the bell markers. Between 2000 and 2006 (the 100th anniversary of the original marker bell), 555 bells were installed. The new bells are cast from a mold of the original marker bells, and are officially maintained by the California Department of Transportation (Caltrans).

A Russian Presence in California

Just as the Spanish Empire spread across the Atlantic to the new world, the Russian Empire expanded across Siberia and the Pacific. The two spheres intersected, briefly, on the North Coast of California.

The Fort Ross settlement was the southernmost outpost of the Russian Empire on the North American continent. The settlement was founded in 1812, and disbanded in 1841. The primary business ventures of the outpost included fur trading, lumber, and shipbuilding.

Meanwhile, the Spanish Empire reached Sonoma in 1823 with the establishment of Mission San Francisco Solano de Sonoma, just 65 miles from Fort Ross. The Russian and Spanish settlements, both far from their home countries, established regular trade to meet their day-to-day needs.

In fact, the disbanding of the Fort Ross settlement was triggered, at least in part, by the secularization of the Spanish missions and the subsequent loss of essential trade. The Fort Ross land was eventually sold by the Russians to John Sutter, whose subsequent discovery of gold in Sacramento triggered the California gold rush.

The buildings at Fort Ross gradually fell into decay. Several of the remaining structures collapsed in the San Francisco earthquake of 1906.

Today Fort Ross is operated as a California State Historic Park. The fort walls and several structures have been rebuilt, and there are regular tours and living history demonstrations.

The Independent Republic of California

The *Bear Flag Revolt* was a popular uprising of settlers in Sonoma, California, against the Mexican government, which at that time controlled California.

The revolt began on June 14, 1848... just a few months after the discovery of gold at Sutter's Mill, near Sacramento. The uprising was short-lived. The participants never formed a government, although they did design a flag: the Bear Flag, which became the model for the California state flag in subsequent years.

The original bear flag was designed by William Todd, a nephew of Abraham Lincoln. The flag was destroyed in the San Francisco earthquake and fire in 1906.

The Republic's first and only president, William B. Ide, ceded control to the United States Army when Major John Fremont arrived with approximately 60 troops. The Republic had lasted just 26 days.

California was formally annexed as a territory of the United States by the Treaty of Guadalupe Hidalgo, in February, 1848, and became a state in 1850.

Compare the original California Bear Flag, designed by William Todd in 1846, with the modern California State flag:

The California Gold Rush

The California gold rush was triggered by the discovery of gold by John Sutter on January 24, 1848.

The subsequent influx of gold seekers (the "49ers") in 1849 transformed California. An estimated 90,000 new settlers arrived in California in 1849 alone. San Francisco became a boomtown, and its population grew from 1,000 to 25,000 in just two years.

Overall, the Gold Rush brought more than 300,000 new settlers to California. The rapidly growing population required an extensive infrastructure. Settlements, roads and railroads were built, and farms and agricultural towns sprang up.

In the rush to stake claims and build new settlements, California Indians were driven from their lands. In the decades after the discovery of gold, over 100,000 California Indians died from starvation, disease and violence.

California became a state in 1850, following a brief period as an independent republic.

The mission era – which had spanned 80 years of California's early history – had come to an end.

1 - San Diego de Alcalá

Founded: July 16, 1769

Founder: Father Junipero Serra

Status: Mission Basilica San Diego de Alcala is an active Roman Catholic Church.

Indian tribes native to surrounding area: Ipai, Tipai, Luiseño, Pai Pai, Kilawa

Location: 10818 San Diego Mission Road, San Diego, CA 92108

Nickname: The Mother of the Missions

San Diego occupies a unique place in California's history, as the site of the first of the California missions, as well as one of four Spanish presidios (military forts).

San Diego was chosen as the base for the construction of the California mission system, largely due to the excellent harbor, which had been discovered by the Spaniards almost 200 years earlier.

The mission, which was originally built adjacent to the Presidio, was moved 6 miles in 1774, to free the padres from the unsavory influence of the soldiers.

In 1776, the mission was attacked by hundreds of Indians who were angered by the Spaniards growing influence. Three of the Spaniards were killed, but the Indians were driven off by the better armed defenders. The soldiers stationed at the Presidio slept through the attack.

Key Events

1769	Mission founded.
1774	Mission relocated, about 5 miles from its original site.
1776	Indian uprising at the mission.
1818	Santa Ysabel Asistencia founded as a sub-mission.
1834	Mission secularized.
1862	Mission returned to the Catholic church.

Visiting the San Diego Mission

Little remains of the original mission structure; today's mission sanctuary was built in 1970, though it retains the traditional mission style.

The mission features a striking *campanario*, or bell wall, featuring five bells. The largest bell, the 1,200 pound Mater Dolorosa, was cast in 1894, using the bronze from five smaller bells sent to the mission in 1794 by the Spanish Viceroy.

Visiting the San Diego Presidio

Although the original Presidio buildings are long gone, Presidio Park, the site of the original fort, is now home to the Junípero Serra Museum. The park is also adjacent to Old Town San Diego, a popular entertainment and shopping area featuring a number of historic buildings and sites.

2 - San Carlos Borromeo de Carmelo

Founded: June 3, 1770

Founder: Father Junipero Serra

Status: Active Roman Catholic Church and Minor Basílica

Indian tribes native to surrounding area: Costanoan, Esselen

Location: 3080 Rio Road, Carmel, CA 93923

Nickname: The Father of the Missions

The second mission was built some 650 miles from San Diego, at Monterey, California.

Like Mission San Diego de Alcalá, the mission at Carmel was easily accessible by sea, with good anchorage in nearby Monterey Bay. Also like San Diego, this second mission was located adjacent to one of four Spanish Presidios (or military forts); a year later the mission was relocated a few miles to what is present day Carmel, California, to avoid the influence of the soldiers stationed at the Presidio.

The presence of the Presidio did not protect the settlement at Monterey. In 1818, the French pirate Hipólito Bouchard attacked the presidio with a large force. The badly outnumbered Spanish defenders withdrew, and Bouchard sacked and burned the Presidio and the town of Monterey. Ironically, the mission was unharmed.

Father Junipero Serra made Mission Carmel the headquarters of the California Mission system (from 1770 to 1803), and Monterey became the first capital of the Alta California territory.

Notably, the mission was also home to California's first library, made up of books brought by Serra and the other padres. Although it began modestly with a few dozen volumes, by 1820 it had over 2,000 books.

Key Events

1770	Mission founded.
1771	California mission headquarters moved to Carmel (until 1815)
1815	California mission headquarters moved to La Purísima Concepción
1818	The Presidio and the town of Monterey are attacked by French pirate Hipólito Bouchard.
1819	California mission headquarters returned to Carmel (until 1824)
1824	California mission headquarters moved to San José
1827	California mission headquarters returned to Carmel (until 1830)
1830	California mission headquarters moved to San José
1834	Mission secularized.
1859	Mission returned to the Catholic Church.
1961	The mission was formally designated a Minor Basilica by Pope John XXIII.

Visiting the Mission

San Carlos Borromeo de Carmelo is often called the most beautiful of the California Missions.

The mission was restored to its present beautiful state in the 1930's. Generous donations have allowed the mission to acquire an extensive collection of historical artifacts. Note the dissimilar bell towers, one with a Moorish-style dome. Many of the nine bells in the larger tower are original.

The main chapel is the burial site of Father Junipero Serra, founder of the California Mission system. There is an elaborate memorial tomb, sculpted from travertine marble in 1924, depicting Father Serra and three other mission pioneers. The Carmel mission Orchard House, built in 1774, is the oldest residence in California.

Visiting the Monterey Presidio

Nothing remains of the Presidio, which once consisted of over 30 buildings, within a walled area 200 feet square. Today the site is home to the US Department of Defense Language Institute, which is not open to the general public.

3 - San Antonio de Padua

Founded: July 14, 1771

Founder: Father Junipero Serra

Status: conference and meeting facility; private retreat

Indian tribes native to surrounding area: Salinan, Esselen, Yokuts

Location: Ft. Hunter-Liggert Reservation, Jolon, CA 93928

Access may be restricted – See *Visiting the Mission*

San Antonio de Padua was built in a broad valley. The excellent farmland made it one of the most prosperous of the California Missions. The holdings included a kiln for firing roof tiles (the first in California), 17,000 head of cattle, a millhouse, a system of reservoirs and flumes for carrying water from the river, and even a room for teaching music to the Indians.

Over time, the mission added a number of additional sites, including ranch builds, corrals, and even a dam on the San Antonio river.

The first recorded marriage in California took place at the mission in 1773, between Margarita de Cortona (and Indian woman) and Juan María Ruiz (a Spanish soldier).

Key Events

1771   Mission founded.

1773   The first officially recorded marriage in California, between Margarita de Cortona and Juan María Ruiz.

1834   Mission secularized.

1863   Mission returned to the Catholic Church.

Visiting the Mission

Mission San Antonio de Padua is the most isolated of the California Missions, in the middle of the Fort Hunter Liggett Military Reservation about half way between U.S. 101 and California Highway 1.

At one time the base gate was guarded, and photo ID was required to enter. The access road has now been rerouted so it does not pass through the secure entry. However, we suggest that you carry your vehicle registration, proof of insurance, and photo ID for each passenger, in case access requirements change in the future. Note that traffic signs and speed limits are strictly enforced by the military police on the base.

San Antonio de Padua is among the best restored of the missions. The church was reconstructed in 1948 under a grant from the William Randolph Hearst Foundation. There are also several historical buildings, a small museum with artifacts, and even a remains of the original water control and irrigation system.

The interior walls feature painted decorations done by the mission Indians. The "music room" shows musical notation and hand symbols used for teaching music.

There has been no development of the land around the mission, so visitors can still see the California "oak scrub" landscape much as it might have appeared to the padres in the 18th century.

4 – San Gabriel Arcángel

Founded: September 8, 1771

Founder: Father Pedro Cambon and Father Angel Somera

Status: Active Roman Catholic Church

Indian tribes native to surrounding area: Tongva, Serrano, Cahuilla

Location: 428 South Mission Drive, San Gabriel, CA 91776

Nickname: The Pride of the Missions.

San Gabriel was one of the busiest of the missions, located at the junction of three major trails. The mission settlement became the seed of modern-day Los Angeles.

The first few years, however, were difficult. One of the mission soldiers raped the wife of a local Indian Chief. The Chief led and attack against the mission, and was shot and killed. The remaining attackers fled but relations between the mission and the surrounding Indians were hostile for many years.

Key Events

1771   Mission founded.

1834   Mission secularized.

1859   Mission returned to the Catholic Church.

Visiting the Mission

The church at San Gabriel Arcángel is one of the most interesting in the mission system. The beautiful façade at the end of the building is actually not an entrance; the doorway to the church is on the long "side" wall.

There is also a *campanario*, or bell wall, featuring six bells, and a museum of mission artifacts. The oldest bells were cast in Mexico City in 1795.

5 - San Luis Obispo de Tolosa

Founded: September 1, 1772

Founder: Father Junipero Serra

Status: Active Roman Catholic Church

Indian tribes native to surrounding area: Chumash, Yokuts

Location: 751 Palm Street, San Luis Obispo, CA 93401

Nickname: Mission of the Valley of Bears

Two years before the founding of Mission San Luis Obispo, an exploratory mission led by Don Gaspar de Portolá was returning to San Diego. The men were short on provisions and half starved when they came signs of bear. They successfully hunted and killed two bear (although one of the soldiers was almost killed in the process), and the resulting meat allowed the men to survive.

In memory of the event, they named the valley *La Cañada de los Osos* (the valley of the bears).

In 1792, when the missions at Carmel and San Antonio were short of provisions, a hunting party was sent back to the valley to hunt. They sent back 9,000 pounds of meat, as well as 25 mule-loads of seeds they gained by trading with the Indians in the valley.

When the hunting party returned, several men were left behind to begin construction of a new mission.

In 1776, a local Indian shot a burning arrow at the thatched roof of the mission, starting a fire that badly damaged several buildings. When the buildings were repaired, the roofs were replaced with locally made tiles, and this practice quickly spread to other missions.

Key Events

1772   Mission founded.

1787   *Asistencia*, or sub-mission, of Santa Margarita de Cortona established.

1834   Mission secularized.

1859   Mission returned to the Catholic Church.

Visiting the San Luis Obispo de Tolosa Mission

The beautiful mission is located in the heart of San Luis Obispo.

Visitors to the mission today can see the adobe church (the *portico* and *campanario* were rebuilt in 1936), an excellent museum, and remnants of the original stone kitchen walls.

6 - San Francisco de Asís

Founded: June 26, 1776

Founder: Father Francisco Palóu

Status: An active Roman Catholic Church and Minor Basilica

Indian tribes native to surrounding area: Ohlone, Costanoan, Miwok, Patwin, Wappo

Location: 3321 16th Street, San Francisco, CA 94114

Nickname: Mission Dolores

The San Francisco bay was discovered accidentally; Spanish ships had previous sailed past the entrance numerous times in the frequent coastal fogs. Reports at the time said the bay "could hold all the armadas of Spain."

Lt. Colonel Juan Bautista de Anza was dispatched from San Diego with a party of over 240 people to establish two missions and a Presidio, or military fort ... one of the four Spanish Presidios built in Alta California.

The first mission was built in a small valley which they names *Arroyo de Los Dolores*, or the Valley of Sorrows, and the name eventually became attached to the mission itself (Mission Dolores).

The inhospitable climate around the mission – cold, damp, and foggy – caused constant health problems, and in later years the mission depended on support from the mission at Sonoma.

In fact, despite the magnificent bay, the settlement at San Francisco struggled until the California Gold Rush, which made the city a boom town, and brought tens of thousands of people and new wealth.

Ironically, the adobe church weathered the great San Francisco earthquake of 1906 with little damage.

Mission Dolores still plays an important role in the civic and cultural life of San Francisco. San Francisco de Asís was granted *basilica* status in 1952 by Pope Pius XII.

Key Events

1776   Mission founded.

1834   Mission secularized.

1857   Mission returned to the Catholic Church.

1952   Minor Basilica status granted by Pope Pius XII.

Visiting the San Francisco de Asís Mission

The *Mission Dolores* church is the oldest intact building in the city of San Francisco, and the only completely intact chapel remaining among the 21 missions. The sturdy, 4-foot-thick adobe walls even withstood the devastating San Francisco earthquake in 1906. The chapel was restored in 1917, and retrofitted for earthquake safety in 1990. (Don't confuse the small mission chapel with the large parish church built immediately next to it.)

There is a cemetery with the remains of padres, soldiers, settlers, and local Indians; it's one of only two cemeteries remaining within the city limits (the other is at the San Francisco Presidio). The cemetery is the final resting place for over 5,000 Indians and Mexican settlers, as well as notables such as Luis Antonio Arguello, the first governor of Alta California, and Lieutenant Moraga, the first commandant of the Presidio.

The grounds also hold gardens and a museum.

Visiting the San Francisco Presidio

The United States Army assumed control of the San Francisco Presidio in 1846, and occupied it as an important military base until 1994.

Today the Presidio is part of the Golden Gate Recreational District. There are numerous historical sites within the large grounds, including fortifications built by the US army to protect the bay. The Officers Club was part of the original Spanish Presidio, and adobe walls have been excavated; it is currently undergoing restoration.

The Presidio also offers hiking and outdoor activities, restaurants, shopping, and numerous businesses.

7 - San Juan Capistrano

Founded: November 1, 1776

Founder: Father Junipero Serra

Status: An active Catholic Church.

Indian tribes native to surrounding area:
Jaunaño, Luiseño, Tongva

Location: 26801 Ortega Highway,
San Juan Capistrano, CA 92675

Nickname: The Jewel of the Missions

San Juan Capistrano was once known as "The Jewel of the Missions" due to the beauty of its buildings and gardens.

Like most of the missions, it began with a modest adobe church. The original chapel was replaced in 1782. This chapel is still standing, and is believed to be the only remaining structure where Father Junipero Serra held mass.

In 1806 the missionaries completed a magnificent, cathedral-like stone church, 180 feet long and 40 feet wide, with a vaulted ceiling and seven domes. Sadly, the most beautiful of all the mission churches stood for only six years. In December, 1812, an earthquake collapsed the church, killing 40 people.

From that point forward, the mission used the older adobe chapel founded by Father Serra.

Key Events

1776   Mission founded.

1818   Great Stone Church destroyed in an earthquake that kills 40 people.

1834   Mission secularized.

1865   Mission returned to the Catholic Church.

Visiting the San Juan Capistrano Mission

Today, visitors to the beautiful and extensive grounds can see the ruins of the stone church, the original adobe church, living quarters, workshops, beautiful gardens, and a museum. The adobe church is believed to be the oldest standing building in California.

The cherry-wood altar was carved in Barcelona, Spain, and is over 300 years old.

A low campanario, or bell wall, features four bronze bells, two of them recovered from the bell tower of the collapsed stone church.

Capistrano may be best known for the fabled swallows, which return to the mission to nest each year on St. Joseph's Day, March 19.

Personal Story

Growing up in Southern California, I heard the story of the Capistrano swallows many times. On my first visit to the mission as a small child, the only birds in sight were the ubiquitous pigeons found at any tourist destination.

For years after, I thought that pigeons were swallows.

8 - Santa Clara de Asís

Founded: January 12, 1777

Founder: Father Junipero Serra

Status: An active Catholic Church and Jesuit University.

Indian tribes native to surrounding area: Ohlone, Costanoan, Miwok, Yokuts

Location: 500 E. Camino Real
Santa Clara, CA 95053

Mission Santa Clara de Asís was the second mission established in the San Francisco Bay area. It was the first California mission to honor a female saint.

Together with the San Francisco Presidio and Mission Dolores (San Francisco de Asís), the mission created a strong Spanish presence and control of the bay area.

At approximately same time, a civilian pueblo, or settlement, was established at nearby San Jose.

Initially, there was friction between the mission and the San Jose community, including disputes over cattle grazing and water rights. Eventually, a four mile road, The Alameda, was built connecting the communities, and leading to better relations. The Alameda is still in use today, a busy multi-lane commuter route.

In 1851, the Jesuit order took possession of the remaining mission buildings, and established a center for higher learning that eventually became Santa Clara University (the oldest university in California).

Key Events

1777   Mission founded.

1836   Mission secularized.

1846   Mission returned to the Catholic church.

1851   Control of the mission is transferred to the Jesuits; it forms the nucleus of Santa Clara University.

Visiting the Santa Clara de Asís Mission

Very little remains of the original mission, aside from a few adobe walls. The current church was constructed in 1929, modeled on a previous structure built in 1825 (and destroyed by fire). It contains a number of statues and furnishings from earlier eras.

There is a tall cross, erected in 1777, across from the church entrance. Also note the four bells in the *companario*; one dates to 1798 and was donated by King Carlos IV of Spain.

The Santa Clara University is a beautiful and historic setting in its own right, and well worth a visit.

9 - San Buenaventura

Founded: March 31, 1782

Founder: Father Junipero Serra

Status: Active Catholic Church.

Indian tribes native to surrounding area:
Ventureño, Chumash, Mojave

Location: 211 East Main Street
Ventura, CA 93001

Nickname: The Mission by the Sea

Mission San Buenaventura was one of the most prosperous and productive of the missions. The mission was regularly visited by whaling ships operating along the Alta California coast. The whaling crews traded for fresh meat and produce from the mission.

However, mission life was never without its dangers.

In 1818, a French pirate, Hippolyte Bouchard, threatened the mission. The mission residents moved their herds and valuables inland several miles for over a month until the danger passed. The following year, a dispute with Mojave Indians became violent; two soldiers and ten Indians were killed.

In the 1970s, the mission was the site of an extensive archeological expedition, which uncovered the remains of a 3,500 year old Indian village, as well as the foundations of early mission buildings.

Key Events

1782   Mission founded.

1818   French pirate Hippolyte Bouchard threatened the mission.

1836   Mission secularized.

1862   Mission returned to the Catholic church, by order of President Abraham Lincoln.

Visiting Mission San Buenaventura

The handsome adobe mission church, restored to something very like its original configuration, can still be seen on Main Street in Ventura. The *companario* contains 5 bells, two of which date to 1781.

There is also a museum featuring many artifacts uncovered by the archeological dig in the 1970s, and a well tended garden with a stone fountain and grotto.

10 - Santa Barbara

Founded: December 4, 1786

Founder: Father Fermin Lasuen

Status: Active Catholic Church

Indian tribes native to surrounding area:
Barbareño, Ineseño, Chumash

Location: 2201 Laguna Street
Santa Barbara, CA 93105

Nickname: The Queen of the Missions

The mission at Santa Barbara was envisioned by Father Junipero Serra as a kind of "bridge" connecting San Luis Obispo de Tolosa and San Gabriel Arcángel. Due to opposition from the governor, who opposed expansion of the mission system, it was not built until after Serra's death.

The mission was protected by the Santa Barbara Presidio, or military fort, built four years earlier, and together with the missions at San Luis Obispo and San Gabriel, solidified Spanish control over the channel area. The Santa Barbara Presidio was the fourth and final military outpost constructed by the Spanish in Alta California (a fifth Presidio, at Sonoma, was built by the Mexican government after independence from Spain).

The mission church, which occupies a central place in the modern city of Santa Barbara, was damaged several times by earthquakes, but survived and was extended and enhanced. A unique and beautiful neoclassical stone façade was added to the church in 1820. A second tower was added in 1831, but collapsed within two years and was subsequently rebuilt.

Mission Santa Barbara relied on the most extensive water system of any of the missions; many of the aqueducts can still be seen, and the route of the water system is still used by the city's water company.

La Misión de La Señora Barbara is the only mission that remained under continuous control by the Franciscan order, so records, artwork, and valuables from several of the other missions were transferred to Santa Barbara.

Key Events

1782	El Presidio Real de Santa Bárbara is founded.
1786	Mission founded.
1820	Neoclassical stone façade added to Church.
1831	Second bell tower added to Church.
1833	California mission headquarters moved to Santa Barbara (until 1946).
1834	Mission secularized.
1865	Mission returned to the Catholic church.

Visiting Mission Santa Barbara

There is a great deal to see at Mission Santa Barbara, including the restored church with its unique façade, an extensive museum and art collection, beautiful gardens, tile fountain, and out-buildings including a mill, tannery, and parts of the original water system.

The Moorish style fountain in front of the monastery wing was created by Antonio Ramírez in 1808.

Visiting the Santa Barbara Presidio

The presidio at Santa Barbara was responsible for the defense of the missions at San Fernando, San

Buenaventura, Santa Barbara, Santa Inés, and La Purísima.

El Presidio de Santa Barbara State Historic Park is operated by the Santa Barbara Trust for Historic Preservation. Visitors can see two restored Presidio buildings as well as later period adobes, ongoing archeological excavations, and a collection of artifacts.

11 - La Purísima Concepción de María Santísima

Founded: December 8, 1787

Founder: Father Fermin Lasuen

Status: a California State Historic Park and "living history" museum

Indian tribes native to surrounding area: Chumash, including Purisimeño, and Ineseño tribes

Location: 2295 Purisima Road
Lompoc, CA 93436

Mission La Purísima Concepción was originally built on the site of the modern city of Lompoc. In December of 1812, the mission 25-year-old was destroyed by an earthquake. Torrential rains and flooding prevented reconstruction on the original site, and the mission was relocated three miles to the North.

The plan of the mission is unique. All of the other California missions were built in the form of a quadrangle; at La Purísima, the buildings are arranged in a line.

During an Indian revolt in 1824, the mission was seized and held by rebels. Soldiers were dispatched from the Monterey Presidio, and bombarded the mission with cannon and rifle fire. The rebels surrendered after three hours; 16 Indians had been killed and many more wounded in the one-sided battle.

After secularization, the mission fell into rapid decline. It was rescued in 1933 by the National Park Service and the Civilian Conservation Corp.

The mission church and many of the outbuildings were completely reconstructed.

Today it is the best example of a working mission community.

Key Events

1787	Mission founded.
1815	California mission headquarters moved to La Purísima Concepción (through 1819)
1824	Indian revolt, suppressed by soldiers from the Monterey Presidio.
1834	Mission secularized.
1865	Mission returned to the Catholic Church.
1934	Mission restored by the National Park Service and the Civilian Conservation Corp (work was completed in 1941).

Visiting La Purísima Mission

La Purísima Mission has been elaborately restored, and hosts over 200,000 visitors each year.

In addition to the restored mission buildings, there is a visitor center, interpretive exhibits, museum, and extensive grounds featuring a network of hiking trails.

The buildings and artifacts provide a fascinating glimpse into the day-to-day life of a working mission. There are kilns for making pottery, looms for weaving, wells and irrigation system, stock pens, living quarters, and more.

The mission is also the site of frequent historical re-enactments. (Check the calendar on the mission website at lapurisimamission.org.)

Personal Note: La Purísima Mission

La Purísima is one of my favorite missions to visit!

The extensive grounds, restorations, and living history re-enactments make it a must-see for any fan of the California mission system.

12 - La Exaltación de la Santa Cruz

Founded: August 28, 1791

Founder: Father Fermin Lasuen

Status: Active Catholic Church

Indian tribes native to surrounding area:
Ohlone, Costanoan, Miwok, Yokuts

Location: 126 High Street
Santa Cruz, CA 95060

Mission Santa Cruz was built in a beautiful location, in the midst of rich agricultural land. By all measures, the mission should have been an outstanding success.

However, when a nearby settlement was established, it quickly attracted a number of failed artisans, petty criminals and unemployed ruffians. Constant friction between the settlement and the mission prevented the mission population from growing.

In 1818, the mission was raided and looted by ex-convicts from the nearby pueblo of Branciforte.

With the smallest population of any of the California missions, Santa Cruz was unable to expand its agricultural production.

Eventually, the settlement expanded into the modern California town of Santa Cruz, while the mission slowly declined.

Key Events

1791   Mission founded.

1818   Mission raided and looted.

1834   Mission secularized.

1859   Mission returned to the Catholic Church by President James Buchanan.

Visiting Mission Santa Cruz

Visitors to the mission can see and adobe neophyte residence, and an interpretive center. There is a relative modern brick church, built is 1889 on the site of the original church.

Nearby there is a 1/3 scale replica of the original mission; the replica was built in 1932.

13 - Nuestra Señora de la Soledad

Founded: October 9, 1791

Founder: Father Fermin Lasuen

Status: Active Catholic Chapel in the town of Soledad.

Indian tribes native to surrounding area: Ohlone, Costanoan, Esselen, Miwok, Yokuts

Location: 36641 Fort Romie Road Soledad, CA 93960

The name of the mission – Our Lady of Solitude – came about due to a misunderstanding. The Spanish missionaries encountered a party of Indians and asked their name. The Indians responded with a word that the Spanish heard as Soledad, or solitude, and this determined the name of the mission.

The location was indeed isolated. During its existence, the mission went through 30 Friars, most of whom requested transfer after a year or less.

The mission was also plagued by repeated flooding from the nearby Salinas River, and a smallpox epidemic killed Indians by the hundreds.

Key Events

1791   Mission founded.

1834   Mission secularized.

1859   Mission returned to the Catholic Church by President James Buchanan.

Visiting the Mission

Today visitors can see archeological excavations, the remains of a few mission buildings, and a small museum.

There is also a simple adobe chapel, built in 1832, and reconstructed in 1955. Colorful paintings and wall decorations can be seen on the interior and exterior walls.

14 - San José

Founded: July 11, 1797

Founder: Father Fermin Lasuen

Status: Active Catholic Church

Indian tribes native to surrounding area:
Ohlone, Costanoan, Miwok, Yokuts,
Patwin, Wappo, Nisenan

Location: 43300 Mission Boulevard
Fremont, CA 94539

Mission San José established the settlement that became the modern city of Fremont. It was the first of a group of five approved as part of a major expansion of the Alta California mission system.

The expansion was intended to reduce the distance between missions, and the need for military escorts when travelling between the missions. The rich lands around the mission were very productive, and it helped to supply livestock, fruit, grain, and olive oil to the surrounding missions.

The mission was, however, troubled by unrest between the Indians and the missionaries. A large-scale Indian uprising in 1828 required over a year, and several military expeditions from the Presidio at San Francisco, to quell.

Plans for a bell tower at the mission were scrapped due to fear of earthquakes. In fact, the mission church and most of the other buildings were destroyed by a major earthquake in 1868.

The current church reconstruction was built in 1982.

Key Events

1797	Mission founded.
1828	Large-scale Indian uprising; quelled by troops for the San Francisco Presidio.
1834	Mission secularized.
1858	Mission returned to the Catholic Church.
1868	Earthquake destroyed adobe church and many nearby buildings.

Visiting Mission San José

Little remains of the original mission. There are a few portions of original walls, the reconstructed church, and small museum (the padres' wing of the original mission). The bell tower houses four original bells.

The *Olive Hyde Art Guild*, across the street from the mission, features special exhibits and the work of local artists.

15 - San Juan Bautista

Founded: June 24, 1797

Founder: Father Fermin Lasuen

Status: Active Catholic Church

Indian tribes native to surrounding area: Mutsun, Yokuts

Location: 406 Second Street
San Juan Bautista, CA 95045

Nickname: The Mission of Music

San Juan Bautista was the second of five missions built as part of a major expansion of the Alta California mission system.

The expansion reduced the distance between missions, and the need for military escorts when travelling between them.

The mission quickly grew and became the core of a prosperous town. It was widely known for its exceptional choir. The mission used a musical notation system developed in Spain where varied colors are used to represent notes; two of the handwritten choir books can be seen in the mission's museum.

In 1812 the current church was completed and dedicated, replacing an earlier adobe chapel. The church is the largest in the mission chain.

The growth of the town was eclipsed by cities like San Jose in 1870, when San Juan Bautista rejected a request from the Southern Pacific Railroad to subsidize the construction of a rail depot. The rail line therefore bypassed the city, and businesses followed.

Key Events

1797   Mission founded.

1812   New church dedicated.

1835   Mission secularized.

1859   Returned to Catholic Church by U.S. President James Buchanan.

Visiting Mission San Juan Bautista

Due to its relatively isolated location, in the small town of San Juan Bautista, much of the mission has been preserved. There is a large adobe church completed in 1812, as well as a beautiful colonnaded walkway along what was once the *convento*, or priests' quarters. There is a museum with an extensive collection of artifacts, and a peaceful garden.

The mission faces a historic town square that is the last remaining Spanish Plaza. There are a number of surviving buildings from Spanish colonial and early American times, including:

- **Castro-Breen Adobe** – A large adobe house, built in 1838 for Mexican General Jose Antonio Castro. It was purchased in 1848 by Patrick and Margaret Breen, survivors of the ill-fated Donner Party, immigrants stranded by snow in the Sierra's during the winter of 1846-47.

- **Plaza Hotel** – Built in 1858 by Angelo Zanetta, it was a thriving hotel during the 1800's.

- **Settlers Cabin w/Gardens** – A typical cabin housing early California settlers.

- **Indian Burial Grounds** – Over 4000 Indians are buried in this cemetery next to the Mission Church.

- **Plaza Hall** – Acquired by Angelo Zanetta in 1868 for use as his private residence.

- **Plaza Stable** – Circa 1870. The stable was built to handle the extensive stage and wagon traffic flowing thru San Juan Bautista.

- **Town Jail** – Circa 1880.

The nearby main street features several galleries, restaurants, and antique stores.

The mission also sits adjacent to a small dirt path – an original portion of *El Camino Real*. The path is 9 feet wide, and there are still ruts from wagon wheels visible in a few places.

The mission was used as a setting for the Alfred Hitchcock film *Vertigo*, released in 1957.

16 - San Miguel Arcángel

Founded: July 25, 1797

Founder: Father Fermin Lasuen

Status: Active Catholic Church and
Franciscan Novitiate

Indian tribes native to surrounding area:
Salinan, Yokuts

Location: 775 Mission Street
San Miguel, CA 93451

Nickname: The Mission on the Highway

Mission San Miguel Arcángel was built near the upper reaches of the Monterey (Salinas) River, to fill the wide gap between Mission San Antonio and Mission San Luis Obispo.

Many of the original buildings, the roof of the church, and a huge quantity of wool, cloth, and grain were lost of a great fire in 1806.

A new, tile-roofed church was completed in 1818. A series of beautiful frescos were painted on the interior walls of the church by talented Mexican artist Estéban Munoz; the frescos can still be seen today.

A *convento* was added in 1822 to house the friars and visiting guests.

Key Events

1797   Mission founded.

1834   Mission secularized.

1859   Mission returned to the Catholic Church.

Visiting Mission San Miguel Arcángel

Visitors can see archeological remains of several adobe buildings, a small museum, and the 1818 adobe church.

The beautiful and colorful frescoes on the church walls are the best-preserved original interior decorations remaining among the California missions.

There is also a unique *campanario*, or bell wall, constructed of adobe and finished with smooth river rocks.

The fountain in front of the mission was added in the 1940s.

17 - San Fernando Rey de España

Founded: September 8, 1797

Founder: Father Fermin Lasuen

Status: Active Catholic Church

Indian tribes native to surrounding area:
Fernandeño, Tataviam, Chumash,
Vanyumé, Kitanemuk

Location: 15151 San Fernando Mission
Boulevard, Mission Hills, CA 91345

The location of Mission San Fernando was chosen for the large springs in the area. The plentiful water supply supported large herds, and the mission eventually became a center for the production of leather goods.

In 1842, a mission rancher found gold particles in nearby Placerita Canyon. Although the gold find was small, it was the first reported gold find in Alta California.

Key Events

1797   Mission founded.

1834   Mission secularized.

1842   Gold found at Placerita Canyon; first known gold find in Alta California.

1861   Mission returned to the Catholic Church.

Visiting Mission San Fernando Rey

The convento (guest house) building features unique river-of-life designs on the doors, and wrought iron locks. There are also two original fountains, as well as a library and museum.

The current church, built in 1974, is an exact replica of a church that was originally built in 1806.

The elaborate altar was carved from walnut and dates to1697. It was imported from Spain by California Missions curator Sir Richard Joseph Menn of the Diocese of Monterey

•

•

18 - San Luis Rey de Francia

Founded: June 13, 1798

Founder: Father Fermin Lasuen

Status: Active Catholic Church

Indian tribes native to surrounding area:
Luiseõ, Ipai, Cupeño, Cahuilla

Location: 4050 Mission Avenue
San Luis Rey, CA 92068

Nickname: The King of the Missions

Named in honor of France's King Louis IX, a Spanish ally, the mission benefited from a local Indian population that was already familiar with the Spanish settlers from the long-established mission communities at San Diego and San Juan Capistrano. It quickly became one of the largest and most prosperous in the mission system, and operated two *asistencias*, or sub-missions.

The beautiful church façade is a perfect example of late mission architecture. The mission complex also featured sunken gardens, a laundry, and a charcoal-filtered spring.

In 1893, a Franciscan novitiate was established on the site; it later became San Luis Rey College. Today it is a retreat and conference center.

Key Events

1798   Mission founded.

1816   *Asistencia*, or sub-mission, of San Antonio de Pala established.

1823   *Asistencia*, or sub-mission, of Las Flores established.

1834   Mission secularized.

1865   Returned to Catholic Church.

1893   Franciscan novitiate established; it later became San Luis Rey College.

Visiting Mission San Luis Rey de Francia

In addition to the beautiful cruciform church and octagonal chapel, visitors will see a sunken garden area with original tiles, a water system, kilns, archeological excavations, and a museum.

19 - Santa Inés

Founded: September 17, 1804

Founder: Father Estevan Tapis

Status: Active Catholic Church

Indian tribes native to surrounding area:
Chumsah and Tulares

Location: 1760 Mission Drive
Solvang, CA 93463

Like many of the later missions, Santa Inés quickly
became successful and prosperous. At times, the mission
hosted three priests.

An earthquake in December, 1812, destroyed the church
and most of the mission buildings. Reconstruction began
immediately. The current church was completed in 1817.

The mission *companario* (bell wall) collapsed several
times, 1911 being the last. Fr. Buckler (who served at the
mission from 1904 to 1920) had the companario
restored shortly after 1911. Unfortunately, the workman
made an unauthorized change, and introduced a fourth
bell.

A restoration in 1947 restored the bell wall to its proper
3-bell configuration..

Key Events

1804   Mission founded.

1824   The largest Indian uprising in mission history began when a soldier beat a neophyte.

1834   Mission secularized.

1862   Returned to Catholic Church.

Visiting Mission Santa Inés

Visitors today will see the church and *convento* buildings, beautiful gardens, archeological digs, and an extensive collection of mission art and architecture.

The museum features bells from 1804, 1808, and 1818, as well as an extensive collection of church vestments, including vestments worn by Junipero Serra.

The view to the east includes the ruins of the mission reservoir system, built in 1820-21, and a largely unspoiled landscape.

20 - San Rafael Arcángel

Founded: December 14, 1817

Founder: Father Vicente de Sarria

Status: Active Catholic Church

Indian tribes native to surrounding area:
Miwok, Wappo, Pomo

Location: 1104 5th Street
San Rafael, CA 94901

The mission was originally built as an *asistencia*, or sub-mission, attached to Mission San Francisco de Asís (at San Francisco).

Many of the neophytes at Mission San Francisco became ill, possibly due to the damp, inhospitable climate there. San Francisco had the highest mortality rate of any of the missions, and thousands there died in epidemics.

The mission at San Rafael was built as a hospital and convalescent home, where the ill could recuperate in the warmer climate of the East Bay.

The mission also expanded the Spanish presence in the San Francisco bay area, which was intended as a bulwark against the perceived threat of the Russian presence at Fort Ross to the North.

The expansion of the mission came during the difficult period of transition from Spanish to Mexican rule. For this reason, the church building was simple and unassuming. It was the first mission to be constructed entirely by native craftsmen.

The builders never added a bell tower or a full quadrangle, features that were typical of many of the earlier and more prosperous missions.

The mission buildings were occupied by General John C. Fremont in 1848, during the Bear Flag Revolt, and thereafter fell into disrepair. A visitor in 1881 reported that nothing remained of the original buildings.

Key Events

1817	Mission founded.
1829	The mission is badly damaged in an Indian attack. Loyal neophytes save the mission friars by hiding them.
1834	Mission secularized.
1848	Mission occupied by General John C. Fremont during the California Bear Flag Revolt.
1855	Returned to Catholic Church
1870	Original mission buildings raised.
1919	A new parish church is built.
1946	A replica of the original mission is built.

Visiting Mission San Rafael

Visitors today can see a replica of the original mission, constructed in 1946, and a small museum. The replica has a facade similar to San Carlos Borromeo de Carmelo, which is not true to the original design.

The museum collection includes three of the original mission bells, hanging from a small wooden bar at the entrance to the chapel (see photo below). Two of the bells were cast in Mexico for the mission; the third was probably acquired in trade from a whaling ship.

21 - San Francisco de Solano

Founded: July 4, 1823

Founder: Father Jose Altimira

Status: California State Historic Park

Indian tribes native to surrounding area:
Miwok, Wappo, Patwin, Pomo

Location: 114 East Spain Street
Sonoma, CA 95476

The final California Mission, and the only mission founded after Mexico's independence from Spain.

The mission was the result of a political compromise between its ambitious founder, Father José Altimira, and church authorities. Altimira founded the mission without church authorization as a replacement for Mission San Francisco de Asís (at San Francisco).

Altimira was allowed to proceed with the construction of the mission, but Mission San Francisco de Asís and Mission San Rafael Arcángel continued to operate as well.

All three missions were intended to act as a barrier to Russian expansion in Alta California, and to that end a Presidio, or military fort, was also built at Sonoma.

However, the feared military conflict never occurred. In fact, as the community at Sonoma grew, the padres and settlers regularly traded with the Russians at Fort Ross.

In later years, Sonoma was the site of the Bear Flag Revolt, which declared Alta California independent from Mexico.

Key Events

1823   Mission founded.

1834   Mission secularized.

1881   The mission is sold to a private party.

1911   A replica of the original mission church is built.

Visiting Mission San Francisco de Solano

The mission is adjacent to a Mexican-style town square, the largest in California, which is still the heart of downtown Sonoma.

Visitors can see a 1913 reconstruction of the mission's adobe chapel, as well as the nearby Presidio.

Visiting the Sonoma Presidio

Visitors can see the barracks and outbuildings of the presidio, now operated as a museum by the State of California.

In additional to the excellent museum, there are several other historic buildings nearby, including Captain Salvador Vallejo's Casa Grande, the Blue Wing Inn, the Sebastiani Theatre, and the Toscano Hotel. Together the many attractions make Sonoma a must-see for anyone interested in California history.

The California Missions Museum

Just a few miles from the mission itself, visitors will find the California Missions Museum (at Cline Cellars).

The museum houses a collection of detailed models of each of the 21 missions, originally constructed for the 1939 World's Fair. There is also a life-size figure of Father Junipero Serra, mission paintings by artists Robert Morris and Henry Nelson, and two stained-glass panels originally housed in Mission San Francisco de Asîs (prior to the 1906 San Francisco earthquake).

Alphabetical List of Missions

Name	Founded	Order	Location
La Purísima Concepción	1787	11	Lompoc
Nuestra Señora de la Soledad	1791	13	Soledad
San Antonio de Padua	1771	3	Jolon (Ft. Hunter-Liggett)
San Buenaventura	1782	9	Ventura
San Carlos Borromeo de Carmelo - P	1770	2	Carmel
San Diego de Alcalá - P	1769	1	San Diego
San Fernando Rey de España	1797	17	Mission Hills
San Francisco de Asís - P	1776	6	San Francisco
San Francisco de Solano - P	1823	21	Sonoma
San Gabriel Arcángel	1771	4	San Gabriel
San José	1797	14	Fremont
San Juan Bautista	1797	15	San Juan Bautista
San Juan Capistrano	1776	7	San Juan Capistrano
San Luis Obispo de Tolosa	1772	5	San Luis Obispo
San Luis Rey de Francia	1798	18	San Luis Rey
San Miguel Arcángel	1797	16	San Miguel
San Rafael Arcángel	1817	20	San Rafael
Santa Barbara - P	1786	10	Santa Barbara
Santa Clara de Asís	1777	8	Santa Clara
Santa Cruz	1791	12	Santa Cruz
Santa Inés	1804	19	Solvang

P – *Presidios*

Missions in Order of Founding

Name	Founded	Order	Location
San Diego de Alcalá - P	1769	1	San Diego
San Carlos Borromeo de Carmelo - P	1770	2	Carmel
San Antonio de Padua	1771	3	Jolon (Ft. Hunter-Liggett)
San Gabriel Arcángel	1771	4	San Gabriel
San Luis Obispo de Tolosa	1772	5	San Luis Obispo
San Francisco de Asís - P	1776	6	San Francisco
San Juan Capistrano	1776	7	San Juan Capistrano
Santa Clara de Asís	1777	8	Santa Clara
San Buenaventura	1782	9	Ventura
Santa Barbara - P	1786	10	Santa Barbara
La Purísima Concepción	1787	11	Lompoc
Santa Cruz	1791	12	Santa Cruz
Nuestra Señora de la Soledad	1791	13	Soledad
San José	1797	14	Fremont
San Juan Bautista	1797	15	San Juan Bautista
San Miguel Arcángel	1797	16	San Miguel
San Fernando Rey de España	1797	17	Mission Hills
San Luis Rey de Francia	1798	18	San Luis Rey
Santa Inés	1804	19	Solvang
San Rafael Arcángel	1817	20	San Rafael
San Francisco de Solano - P	1823	21	Sonoma

P - *Presidios*

Mission Timeline

Year	Mission	Event
1769	San Diego de Alcalá	Mission founded
1770	San Carlos Borromeo de Carmelo	Mission founded
1771	San Carlos Borromeo de Carmelo	California mission headquarters moved to Carmel (through 1815)
1771	San Antonio de Padua	Mission founded
1771	San Gabriel Arcángel	Mission founded
1772	San Luis Obispo de Tolosa	Mission founded
1773	San Antonio de Padua	The first recorded marriage in California , between Margarita de Cortona (an Indian woman) and Juan María Ruiz (a Spanish soldier).
1774	San Diego de Alcalá	Mission relocated about 5 miles from its original site, to free the padres from the 'unsavory' influence of the soldiers at the Presidio.
1776	San Diego de Alcalá	Indian uprising at the mission.
1776	San Francisco de Asís (Mission Dolores)	Mission founded
1776		13 American colonies declare independence from Great Britain.
1776	San Juan Capistrano	Mission founded
1777	Santa Clara de Asís	Mission founded
1782	San Buenaventura	Mission founded
1782	Santa Barbara	El Presidio Real de Santa Bárbara is founded
1783		American Revolutionary War ends; United States granted independence under the Treaty of Paris.

Year	Mission	Event
1786	Santa Barbara	Mission founded
1787	La Purísima Concepción	Mission founded
1787	San Luis Obispo de Tolosa	Santa Margarita de Cortona Asistencia founded as a sub-mission.
1791	Santa Cruz	Mission founded
1791	Nuestra Señora de la Soledad	Mission founded
1797	San José	Mission founded
1797	San Juan Bautista	Mission founded
1797	San Miguel Arcángel	Mission founded
1797	San Fernando Rey de España	Mission founded
1798	San Luis Rey de Francia	Mission founded
1804	Santa Inés	Mission founded
1806	San Juan Capistrano	The Great Stone Church, a magnificent cathedral, is completed. The cathedral is destined to stand just six years before being destroyed in an earthquake.
1810		Mexican War of Independence begins.
1812	San Juan Capistrano	The Great Stone Church, constructed in 1806, is destroyed in an earthquake; 40 people are killed.
1812		Russian settlement established at Fort Ross.
1815	La Purísima Concepción	California mission headquarters moved to La Purísima Concepción (through 1819)
1816	San Luis Rey de Francia	San Antonio de Pala Asistencia founded as a sub-mission.
1817	San Rafael Arcángel	Mission founded

Year	Mission	Event
1818	San Diego de Alcalá	Santa Ysabel Asistencia founded as a sub-mission.
1818	San Carlos Borromeo de Carmelo	The Monterey Presidio and the town of Monterey are attacked by French pirate Hipólito Bouchard.
1818	Santa Cruz	Mission raided and looted.
1819	San Carlos Borromeo de Carmelo	California mission headquarters moved to Carmel (through 1824)
1821		Mexican independence from Spain granted under the terms of the Plan of Iguala.
1823	San Francisco de Solano	Mission founded. This is the final California Mission, and the only mission founded after Mexico's independence from Spain.
1823	San Luis Rey de Francia	Las Flores Asistencia founded as a sub-mission.
1824	San José	California mission headquarters moved to San José (through 1827)
1824	La Purísima Concepción	Indian revolt, suppressed by soldiers from the Monterey Presidio.
1827	San Carlos Borromeo de Carmelo	California mission headquarters moved to Carmel (through 1830)
1830	San Gabriel Arcángel	San Bernardino Asistencia founded as a sub-mission.
1830	San José	California mission headquarters moved to San José (through 1833)
1833	Santa Barbara	California mission headquarters moved to Santa Barbara (through 1846)
1834		Missions secularized by the Mexican government.

Year	Mission	Event
1841		Russian Settlement at Fort Ross officially disbanded; the land is sold to John Sutter, whose subsequent discovery of gold in Sacramento triggered the California gold rush.
1848		California Bear Flag Revolt against Mexican rule.
1848	San Rafael Arcángel	Mission occupied by General John C. Fremont during the California Bear Flag Revolt.
1848		John Sutter discovers gold, triggering the California gold rush.
1850		California becomes the 31st US state.
1851	Santa Clara de Asís	Control of the mission transferred to the Jesuits, to form the nucleus of a Santa Clara University (which continues to operate today).
1893	San Luis Rey de Francia	Franciscan novitiate established at the mission; it later became San Luis Rey College.

26010518R00043

Made in the USA
San Bernardino, CA
16 November 2015